When I Die
Bury Me
— *as a* —
Muslim

When I Die Bury Me *as a* Muslim

EVERY SOUL WILL TASTE DEATH

JAMELLA A. JIHAD

ISBN: 979-8-89031-770-4 (sc)
ISBN: 979-8-89031-771-1 (hc)
ISBN: 979-8-89031-772-8 (e)

THE EWINGS
PUBLISHING

One Galleria Blvd., Suite 1900, Metairie, LA 70001
(504) 702-6708

IN LOVING MEMORY

SUNNY (LEAH) HENTON

CONTENTS

INTRODUCTION

كُلُّ نَفْسٍ ذَائِقَةُ الْمَوْتِ ۗ وَنَبْلُوكُم بِالشَّرِّ وَالْخَيْرِ فِتْنَةً ۖ وَإِلَيْنَا تُرْجَعُونَ

Every soul will taste death.
And We test you with evil and with good as trial;
and to Us you will be returned.
Quran: 21:23

The purpose of this small handbook is to help families who have family members that have chosen Islam as their way of life. This easy to read booklet should answer most common ask questions.

Islam stands on five principles known as five pillars

1. Shahada: Testimony of faith
2. Salat: Prayer
3. Zakat: Charity
4. Sawm: Fasting
5. Hajj: Pilgrimage to Mecca

These principles are obligatory for every Muslim, ordered by Allah. 34 years ago, I'd taken my shahadah (testimony of faith) to Islam; I bear witness that there is no God, except Allah, and Muhammad is the last Messenger (may peace and blessing be upon him). I was only 18 when I decided to take a leap of faith. I am praying that I will live the remaining of my life as a Muslimah, and I am praying that I die as a Muslimah, and be buried as a Muslimah. This is the decision one will make when becoming a Muslim man or woman. This is a confirmation of a Muslims faith.

When a person chooses a faith, it's likely that they have chosen to be buried the way in their faith. In many cases the person(s) who are not a part of that faith, may or may not accept the faith or the way their love one decide to live their life or the way they choose to be bury. Sadly to say that many people do not accept when people does something different from themselves, however, it's the right of an responsible adult to decide on their faith and how they would like to be bury and in my opinion regardless of what one may feel, we shouldn't never take that right out of a person's hand unless the person have given you the right to do so or you have power of attorney.

When my dear beloved Leah passed away, I made my intentions to write this book that I had promised that I would write this book for families who have none Muslim family members in hope it will give one a better understanding in the way their love one(s) decide to live out their life, and to help relatives accept the decision that their family member(s) have made to be buried as a Muslim. In many cases no one expects to out live a love one, or and in some cases we believe we have time to inform our family members about our life and how we want to be bury. It's difficult for one to accept the decision of a love one either before they die or after they die. It become imperative for every human being handle their affairs before their death. We owe it to ourselves to make sure we inform our family and community how we want to be bury. This small handbook should help bring comfort to your family or to you if you have a love one who chooses Islam as their way of life while they are living or after they pass away. I hope and pray this will help you better understand the Islamic burial as well as one Islamic life.

Throughout the book you will see that I reference God to Allah both mean the same, one means God in the English language and Allah means God in Arabic language. When we Muslim says Allah we are talking about the Creator of the Universe of all things. Many people may call themselves "god" or worship the devil they may call the devil their "god". To make it clear who we're referencing I will say Allah so we are clear.

In today's society there are so many wicked people who have high-jacked Islam, that have tried to make people believe we are worshiping an unknown being. It is so important to be perfectly clear, we are talking about the Creator who Created Adam and Hawah (Eve), we are talking about the God of Abraham, Moses, Jesus, Noah, Jacob, John, David, Salomon, Petter, Paul, Muhammad (may peace be upon them all)!

Respecting one way of life doesn't mean one have to accept the way one chooses to live their life. Many people practice unknown faiths or lifestyles that others may not agree with, even with this being said, a person who dies be we like it or not we should respect the fact that they have the right to be buried according to their faith. In so many cases people do not leave behind a Living Will, it is so importance for one to leave a Will behind especially when one is concern if it's a possibility a family member(s) will not carry out his or her desire to be buried in accordance to their faith. Way to often people dies without preparation, no will, no insurance, leaving their death for their next of kin to handle or their religion institutions. Death is very serious even more than living in my humble opinion. Death is inevitable and once death happens there is nothing one can do or change it, unlike living people are blessed with opportunities to repent, correct and is given a free will to choose. But once you die your "free will" ends. Without proper preparation and instructions you're taking a risk in relying on others to bury you the way you will like to be bury. We shouldn't totally depend on others to bury us in accordance to the way we wish to be buried. This is why it's important to communicate with your family and explain your way of life and how you will like to be bury.

Preparing for death is something that many people don't plan for especially many young adults, most people live as if they will live forever, this is not reality, and our reality is the fact that we all will die. What one does not understand is what happens beyond death? Many people believe so many things about death however no one truly know exactly what happens after one dies other than the body goes back to the earth. In this book you will learn what Muslim believes happens after death. Then you have people who don't worry about death and do not believe nothing takes place after death and some believe they will never die even when death takes them. If they are truthful to their claim, why want they raise themselves back to life or their love one back to life after they dies?

Allah wills this small book will bring comfort and light to family and friend in the departure of a Muslim love ones and answer most commonly ask questions the social life of a Muslim.

Enjoy

Jamella Jihad

MUSLIM BURIAL

وَاتَّقُوا يَوْمًا تُرْجَعُونَ فِيهِ إِلَى اللَّهِ ۗ ثُمَّ تُوَفَّىٰ كُلُّ نَفْسٍ مَا كَسَبَتْ وَهُمْ لَا يُظْلَمُونَ

And fear a Day when you will be returned to Allah.
Then every soul will be compensated for what it earned,
and they will not be treated unjustly.
Quran 2:281

Q: Who should be call when a love's one dies?

A: See Contact Information on page 32

Q: Is autopsy allowed in Islam?

A: Islamically autopsy is not permissible in Islam. However, it's the law in case of murder.

Q: Can a Muslim be cremated?

A: No, it's not permissible for a Muslim to get cremated

Q: Can a Muslim get embalm?

A: No, it's not permissible for a Muslim to be embalmed or have any kind of cosmetology. Embalmed is only permissible if there is a medical reason by law.

Q: Can a the decease body be place in a coffin

A: Depending on how one dies will determined if a casket is best. However, most Muslims are buried without caskets or vaults. Without these items the body will not be preserve and this will allow the body to return to the earth properly.

Preparation for Salat al-Janazah (Islamic funeral prayer)

Q: **What are the steps to preparing the body for burial.**

A: **1.** Once it is known that a love one as passed, they will immediately contact local Imam. If love one has a Will then the family member or person who was left as executive of estate is usually the one who will make contact with Imam or Muslim companion of the deceased. If there is a living spouse then the spouse will make proper arrangements. In the event there wasn't a spouse for Muslim family members such as Muslim children and if the deceased did not leave a Living Will, I would recommend a call be put in to local Imam, from this point the Imam will assist in making arrangements. Usually the body is buried within 3 days due to the fact that the body isn't preserved.

2. Once the body is released to the Funeral Home from hospital, Corners, or from their home. Depending on the decease gender the family will make contact with the person(s) who has knowledge of washing and shrouding the body. Usually men will handle the washing of the male bodies and women will handle washing the female bodies, this type of washing is call ghusl (ablution).

3. Once the body is washed and shroud, family members are allowed to see their love one after shroud. Depending on the family, each family are different and Muslim family tries to stay as close to the Sunnah of our beloved Prophet Muhammad pbuh, as long as it is not displeasing to Allah. Most Muslim family members give their non-Muslim family members the opportunity to observe and or participate in assisting in preparing the decease for their funeral. Usually the face is exposed for the short viewing for the family members to see and immediately covered afterward. There is no open viewing before Janaza i.e. wake or at funeral service.

4. Depending on the Masjid, or the person who are in charge of conducting the janaza (immediate family members) some will hold the funeral outside and some will hold the funeral inside. In Islam there are many different school of thoughts, and there are many different cultures therefore we try to stick closed to the Sunnah of our beloved Prophet Muhammad (peace be upon him) as possible. May Allah be pleased!

Islamic funeral is short, the prayer is performed in congregation, 3 rows are made if more than 3 rows, then it should be odd numbers 3, 5, 7 rows if necessary for men and women. Women will start their rows behind the brothers, the brothers will be in front of the women.

Depending on the community the person who is put in charged usually explains the procedure and in some cases other Imams will allow family members to speak briefly. Once again this will be discussed between all parties involved in carrying out the wishes of the deceased. In some cases the deceased may have left a will, this person may have insisted that there is no obituary, no talking, and would only like the prayer to be perform and their body taken straight to the grave. The Imam will explain what will take place.

Many American follow some traditions such as providing an obituary, and having a repast that will take place at the family place of choice. In accordance to Islamic burial, majority of the Muslim Janaza has limited conversation in respecting the deceased and then the body is rushed to the grave.

5. Performing the Janaza prayer, the shrouded body is usually placed in front of the brothers facing the Ka'bah (towards east). At this point the Imam will announced to make sure there are odd numbers for the prayer. The Imam will explain that we will only be standing in Qiyaam (stand upright) and facing the Ka'bah. The Imam will excuse those who are not Muslim to stay seated or move off to the side while the Muslims pray for their loves ones.

6. The Imam will let the believers know that there will be four Takbir and each Takbeer is as followed:

Takbir One: Al-Fatiha –The Opening Prayer
Takbir Two: At-Tashahud- Prayers for the Prophets
Takbir Three: Prayers for the Deceased
Takbir Four: Prayers for those who remain behind

After Takbir Four and prayers for those who remain behind will Salaam out from right to left.

7. The shrouded body is place in a grave without a casket or vault. The body isn't reserved. A prayer is offer at the graveside after the body is covered in the grave. This concludes the end of the obligatory Janaza prayer for the deceased this is obligatory for every Muslim to make sure their deceased is laid to rest properly truly he/she depends on the believers to carry out this task. In the Islamic faith, it is stated when the last person leave the grave, the body will sit up and the Angels will asked the deceased questions: 1. Who is your Lord, 2. What is your religion? 3. Who is your Prophet?

MUSLIM SOCIAL LIFE

In this next section of this book we offer
some questions and answers to the Most asked
Questions by Non-Muslims who seek knowledge and
understanding about Muslim and their Islamic faith.

Q: If my son or daughter becomes Muslim how will this affect his relationship with his parents?

وَقَضَى رَبُّكَ أَلَّا تَعْبُدُوا إِلَّا إِيَّاهُ وَبِالْوَالِدَيْنِ إِحْسَانًا ۚ إِمَّا يَبْلُغَنَّ عِندَكَ الْكِبَرَ أَحَدُهُمَا أَوْ كِلَاهُمَا فَلَا تَقُل لَّهُمَا أُفٍّ وَلَا تَنْهَرْهُمَا
ـ وَقُل لَّهُمَا قَوْلًا كَرِيمًا

And your Lord has decreed that you not worship
except Him, and to parents, good treatment. Whether
one or both of them reach old age [while] with you, say
not to them [so much as], "uff," and do not repel them
but speak to them a noble word.
Qu'ran 17:23

A: Parents are very important in Islam especially mothers. If your son or daughter becomes a Muslim they must respect you and do right by you, obey you as long as you don't tell them to worship any deity other than Allah or commit any kind of sins that are forbidden by Allah. Other than that it is important to know your Muslim son or daughter should be setting a good example for his non-Muslim family members.

Q: My Muslim daughter says that I cannot come into her home because I am not a Muslim.

A: If your daughter is not allowing you in the house it's shouldn't be because you're not Muslim, it maybe for other reasons.

Because Allah tells us how to treat our mother and father, if she not allowing you in her home she should tell you exactly why?

Q: **Is Allah another God other than the one Christians or Jews worshiped?**

A: To better answer this question let me first say when a Muslim says Allah they mean no other entity other than the Creator of the Universe. In most Arab speaking countries where there are Christians or Jews the majority says "Allah". Therefore when a Muslim says Allah it's the Arabic word for God. Just like in many languages they may say another word for God.

Q: **What Holy Book Do Muslims Reads**

A: Qur'an and you will hear some pronounce it Koran

Q: **Can a non-Muslim read the Qur'an?**

A: Yes, it is encourage for you to read the Qur'an and if you have any questions please asked someone who is very knowledgeable of the Qur'an.

Q: Do Muslim believe in Jesus Christ (may peace be upon him)?

وإذ قال الله يا عيسى ابن مريم أأنت قلت للناس اتخذوني وأمي إلهين من دون الله ۝ قال سبحانك ما يكون لي أن أقول ما
ليس لي بحق ۝ إن كنت قلته فقد علمته ۝ تعلم ما في نفسي ولا أعلم ما في نفسك ۝ إنك أنت علام الغيوب

And [beware the Day] when Allah will say,
"O Jesus, Son of Mary, did you say to the people,
'Take me and my mother as deities besides Allah ?'"
He will say, "Exalted are You! It was not for me to
say that to which I have no right. If I had said it,
You would have known it. You know what is
within myself, and I do not know what is within
Yourself. Indeed, it is You who is
Knower of the unseen.
Qu'ran 5:116

A: Yes, Muslim does believe in Jesus Christ the son of Mary (Maryam- in Arabic). Some say that Jesus (pbuh) is God, however, Islam teaches us that Allah has no partners, sons or daughters and that Allah is the Creator of all things. We believe that Jesus (pbuh) like many other Prophets was sent to their people (Jews). However, the Jews do believe that the Jesus will come to earth in an appointed time though they claimed to kill Jesus on the cross. It was another people who was the followers of Jesus Christ (pbuh) who then called themselves Christians after Christ and those who believe

Jesus died also believe Jesus died for their sins. Where Muslims believe that Jesus didn't die, but was raised to Allah and like the Jews and Christians, Jesus (pbuh) will return to earth at an appointed time and Jesus (pbuh) will stand with the righteous and those who believe in his teaching, and those who didn't worship him. This is part of what Muslim believes. So it is safe to say for the sake of argument yes, we do believe that Jesus (pbuh) was one of the greatest Prophets and like other Prophets everyone was sent to their people.

Q: **Does Muslim believe in Adam and Eve?**

A: Yes, Muslim believes that Allah created Adam and then He Created a mate for Adam from Adam's rib and her name is Eve (Hawa-Arabic). We believe Adam and Hawa was lead astray by the shaitan (satan) that convinces them to go towards the forbidden tree in which Allah told them not go near.

Q: **My family member decided to become Muslim, what should I know about their new way of life and how will it affect our family?**

A: When a person make a decision to become Muslim they are saying that they believe in the Islamic Monotheism, which begins with the five (5) pillars of Islam and each pillar is obligatory

1. Testimonial of Faith
2. Five (5) Daily Prayers
3. Zakat (Charity)
4. Sawn (Fasting)
5. Hajj (Pilgrimage)

The testimonial is when a person says: I bear witness that there is no God except Allah and Muhammad is the last Messenger. After this testimony the person will work towards righteousness and the remaining of the 4 pillars.

The five daily prayers is made five (5) times a day seven (7) days a week. The five prayers are name:

1. Fajr, before the rise of the sun
2. Zhur (afternoon prayer)
3. Asr (mid-day prayer)
4. Magrib (sunset – prayer)
5. Isha (night prayer)

Usually it takes the average person 5 minutes to make each obligatory prayer. Means that the person will give 25 minutes a day to their Lord. No this isn't strange this is a good thing to practice giving Allah the praises and Glory especially to balance out ones life. Note: when you can give a job, or family or friends 8 – 12 hours work day total 15-20 hours a day to someone other than Allah, it is good to be able to give 25 minutes of your time to a obligatory prayer that Allah demanded. To learn when the Muslim prayer time you can visit: http://www.islamicfinder.org/world.php.

If a Muslim decides to make extra prayers it's a blessing.

Fasting: Muslim is obligated to fast during the month of Ramadan. This mean that a person who are Muslim and are fasting during Ramadan wake up an hour or two before Fajr to eat a small meal or breakfast and the person will discontinue to eat when the first call to prayer. The person will not eat or drink until the first call for Magrib prayer is made the person will break their fast usually with a date and with water then make prayer. Some may eat a small meal before eating dinner. Then Magrib prayer will be made after the prayer, then one will eat dinner. This is done for 30 days until Ramadan the end of Ramadah. During this time Muslims work towards completing the Holy Qu'ran. Most communities come together to have iftar (dinner) at their local Masjids, and some read Qu'ran together. After Isha prayer, a sunnah prayer is made which is call Tahwir prayer. It is forbidden to have sexual relations with your spouse during fasting hours. It is also encourage to stay away from those harmful things that are unlawful i.e smoking. Note : For

Muslims who are not able to fast can give zakat or feed poor people.

Zakat: Is known as alms giving, it is a percentage of a person wealth, this obligatory for every Muslim.

Pilgrimage: For a Muslim it is when a Muslim go to Mecca, to circulate around the Kaba and the visiting of Arafat this is hajj, its obligatory for every able-bodied Muslim.

Fasting and Hajj is the only exception where Allah make exception for the sick and the poor. This is where Allah has allowed Muslims with these conditions to feed someone, or a family member can make the hajj and fast on the person behalf.

Q: Can Muslim marry outside of their faith?

A: Only Muslim men are allowed to marry non-Muslim women of another faith. The reason it is permissible for a man to marry a non-Muslim woman is because a man is the head of his household and usually it is the woman who follows her husband way of life. In some cases Muslim men who marry non-Muslim woman doesn't force the person to accept Islam and in some cases non-Muslim women do not change their faith. It is recommended for a Muslim man who is considering to marry a non-Muslim women is to a.

wait until she become Muslim or b. not to marry her if he is leading his household to practice his way of life (Islam).

Q: **Can a Muslim drink alcohol?**

A: No, it is unlawful for a Muslim to drink alcohol, it is forbidden by Allah. Though alcohol is legal in many countries it still if forbidden by Allah. We can agree that alcohol is the caused of many illnesses and has caused many deaths. When one is intoxicated they are unaware of the things that they are doing are things that they have done. For a Muslim who believes in Allah and the last days they will stay away from such substances of all kind that will cause intoxication of the mind. Intoxication of the mind will cause man to forget about their covenant with Allah.

Q: **Can a Muslim have a girl friend or boy friend?**

A: It is not permissible to have relations with the opposite sex other than your wife or husband. But if you asking if a Muslim can have a non-Muslims for friends, yes however, it is best for people of the opposite sex not to put themselves in uncomfortable positions or in positions that will leave to be displeasing to Allah.

Q: Do Muslims celebrate holidays?

A: Muslims celebrate only two holidays Eid Al-Fitr is celebrated at the end of Ramadan (fasting) and Eid Al-Adha is celebrated on the 10th day of Dhu al-Hijjah (after the Hajj). Though there are some people of the Islamic faith who may participate in non-religious holidays such as Thanksgiving. Many Muslims who practice the Sunnah of Muhammad (pbuh) do not celebrate any other Holidays than these two EID.

Q: Are there other meats that are forbidden to Muslim other than pork and if yes what are they?

A: There are Animals that are unlawful for Muslims to eat, with hoof, claws, is forbidden for Muslims, and people who follow the book, of the Jews and Christian to eat pork or any animal with claws, hooves or animals that are slaughter in another name outside the name of Allah. Pork is a known as swine, which is in the Old Testament; man should stay away from swine. There are many scientific reasons why human being shouldn't eat pork and it is proof that this meat is very unhealthy.

Q: Do Muslims believe all non-Muslims are going to hell?

A: No, a Muslim cannot say who are going to hell or to heaven. Only Allah knows who are going to hell or to heaven. It is stated that a man can be closer to hellfire and enter into paradise and visa/versa. A man can be closes to paradise and enter into hellfire this includes all people. Only Allah knows those who He will turn their hearts. But to judge, we only can judge one by their actions but even with this, at the last hour a man can change his ways and die and enter in to paradise or enter into hell. Only Allah knows who will die a believer or a disbeliever.

Q: Do Muslim believe that all non-Muslims are disbelievers (kafirs).

A: No, it is clear who is a believer or a disbeliever by his or her actions in regards to believing in Allah or not. There are some people who religion requires them to worship the devil, it is clear that they are a disbeliever in Allah. And you have some people who has partnered gods up with Allah, it is clear they are disbelievers. Unless they verbally say they worship something other than Allah it is clear they are a disbeliever. A Muslim can be a disbeliever, a Muslim who does not follow the laws of Allah i.e. pray obligatory prayer is a disbeliever until the person turn to Allah in repentance.

Q: **I am a non-Muslim if my Muslim boyfriend dies he told me that he want to be buried as a Muslim.**

A: What constitute a boy and girl friend in America? Depending on the state of your relationship one who you considered a friend be boy or girl with no intimate relations or a person that you are intimate with i.e sexual relations.

Let assume this is a person you are intimate with. Do your "boyfriend" attend a Mosque? If not, then you should encourage him to bring honor to himself, you and to your family he owes this to you as a Muslim. When a Muslim or non-Muslim sins, in the time of their sinful acts they are a disbeliever. Until they both turned to Allah in repentance seeking forgiveness and discontinue the sin, one continue to sin they will remain as a disbeliever. So it's important to remind him that he owes it to himself and to you and your family to discontinue the sin and marry you. Fornication is a sin in all religion. It's important for a Muslim to establish him or herself in a community in the event that he or she dies and it's just as important for him or her to leave a WILL so his wish can be carried out.

Q: **My Muslim brother committed suicide and I was told that no one can attend his jannaza so I buried him the way in which my Christian family member get buried. I feel bad that I couldn't carry out his wishes, how can I help others to carry out their family wishes.**

A: Suicide is a permanent solution to a temporary problem, however in Islam your brother still could have had a Janaza however, depending on the circustances around his death some will not follow him to his grave or pray for him because he died as a disbeliever. In Islam we are taught to not kill innocent people or ourselves. Killing is permissible, if its self-defense or war, in many cases there are some people who suffer from severe depression or is known to have a mental illness, which medication may provoke suicide, with this being known Allah is MOST MERCIFUL. Only Allah knows a person heart and conditions. Allah is forgiving, but make no mistake its must be known that a person suffers from mental illness. But a person who intentionally commit suicide because he think this is the way to die to get closer to Allah or to cause harm and death to himself or herself or to others unlawfully in the name of religion they died as a disbeliever. Then we shouldn't follow him or her to be buried or pray for this person. Though arrangements maybe made for this person to be buried traditionally (as a Muslim)

Q: My relative died without a WILL, though she was a Muslim but not married and no children, she separated herself from the families, we didn't know her friends or the community she was a part of so her mother buried her the traditional way. What should have been done in a case like this?

A: Sadly that your love one was known in the family as a Muslim and the family took responsibility to bury her. What should have been done is for someone to reach out to a local Mosque in the area and let them know that a relative died as the only Muslim in your family, and you want to bury him or her in accordance to their faith. Then it becomes the obligation of the community to see that he/she is buried in accordance to the Islamic faith and the Sunnah of our Beloved Prophet (pbuh).

This is why it is important that people who confess to be a Muslim handle their affairs immediately. It is a Muslim obligation to put their burial in place and explain to their non-Muslim family members, especially if the person has no other family members who are Muslims.

Q: Why a Muslim must be buried within 3 days?

A: If a human being are not embalm the body cannot remain out before autolysis began to take place. Autolysis is known as self-digestion. This begins after the person dies. A Muslim should be buried within 3 days due to the fact that Muslims are not preserved. Meaning that we are not embalm nor do we have autopsy, due to these reasons other than being ordered by Allah to be buried within 3 days before the body began the stages of decaying. Out of respect for the decease the decease should be bury before body start decaying.

Q: Do Muslim donate their organs?

A: Many reasons it was said that Muslims shouldn't be donors, nowadays there are some scholars who states that Muslims can be organ donors, there are some strict guidelines, we must thoroughly researched before making that decision. Again a Muslim should take care of these things before they return to Allah.

Q: My son had died as a Muslim without a Will, his wife is Christian, she wants to bury him as a Christian though he stressed to us both to make sure he is buried as a Muslim. My question what could I have done differently if I didn't have right over his affairs?

A: Unfortunately nothing without a Will. You hear about cases like this and unfortunately if your son didn't take care of his affairs before he died its not to much could have been done outside of trying to reason with his wife. I will suggest having an Imam speak with the wife and to the family together. Hopefully, this will change the wife mind about burying her love one other than a Muslim. Most times a person may not practice Islam according to the guidelines of their faith but when it comes to death their wishes is to be burry as their faith. Its important for men and women of the Islamic faith to put their affairs in order especially when they are married to people who does not share the same belief or wishes as their own.

Q: Can Muslim Be Cremated

A: No, it is against the Islamic faith for a Muslim to be cremated.

Q: **Can we have a traditional service like a chorus, an a minister from both Muslim and Christian faith, though we will bury him/her in the Islamic Tradition?**

A: No, according to the tradition of our beloved Prophet (pbuh) we are rush to the grave right after prayer. In some cases people will have Imam to explain to the family what is about to take place and why, then prayer will follow and the body is rush to the grave. **See burial on page**

Q: **Are my Muslim family allowed to attend my church and I attend her/his place of worship?**

A: Usually when a person becomes Muslim they are coming from another faith, therefore the person doesn't intend to return, due to the different of practice. However, some family members may visit the church of their parents out of respect or during a funeral. Sometimes a parent may invite a Muslim family to a program and visa/versa. However, communication is very important, no one should impose their belief on one another unless asked about their faith.

It is encourage for a Muslim family member to invite their family to their place of worship so they can

Q: Do you have to change your birth name when you becomes Muslim?

A: No it's not obligatory to change your birth name when you become a Muslim. Most time people change their name to names that are meaningful. During the time when Muslims and Africans was taken from their country they were stripped from their names and given the name of their slave holder. Because of this knowledge many African American Muslim choose the names of their ancestors, which were beautiful African/Middle Eastern names and many Quranic and Biblical names. Many Muslims name themselves and their children after names in the Holy Quran same as Christians and Jews.

Q: Why does Muslim women cover from head to toe and why does some Muslims covers their faces and others do not?

A: Muslim women are ordered to cover their heads and dress modest as well as men should dress modest. Religion of old, people always dressed modest and covered their heads. Women wore long dresses and skirts. It's not obligatory to cover your face mean wearing a veil. You can find many Muslim women who do wear the veil. Nowadays you can find Muslim women in non-Islamic country who may not dress in the traditional dress (Middle Eastern clothes). However, this doesn't means they are not Muslims are following the five pillars of Islam.

Q: Is it permissible for a Muslim man to marry more than one woman?

A: In the Islamic faith it is permissible for a man to have up to four wives, and in some countries it is permissible by law of that country for men to legally be married to more than one wife. However, in the United States though Islam is permissible as is any other religion, United States do not allow no religion to have more than one wife. Though you will find there are many men who has more than one wife in some religion. Though people frown when you speak of being in a polygyny marriage, most people will accept or participate in fornication or adultery before accepting a man maintaining more than one wife lawfully in the eyes of God.

Q: I have a Quran with Arabic writing, how can I learn to speak the language.

A: There are many mosques' that have classes, and you can learn Arabic online.

Q: Do Muslim children have to attend Islamic schools?

A: No, however, we recommend for children to attend Islamic schools in your area or allow your children to be homeschool. Many religious family prefer to send their children to private schools or schools of their faith due to the nature of public schools.

There are many questions one may have about the Islamic faith, please feel free to contact your local Mosque.

GLOSSARY

Allah: Arabic word for God

Shahada: Testimony of faith or confession of faith

Salat: Prayer

Zakat: Almsgiving

Sawm: Fasting during the month of Ramadan, this fast is obligatory

Hajj: Pilgrimage to Mecca

Jahannam: Arabic word for Hellfire

Shaitan: Arabic word use for the Devil

Jinns: Good and bad spirit of an unseeing being. Human jinn is one that had a evil spirit about themselves.

Qi'yam: Upright standing position in prayer

Kaba: A structured that was built by Prophet Abraham (peace be and blessing be upon him) Muslims circulate around this structure during hajj.

CONTACT INFORMATION

You can look up the masjid that is closes to you https://www. salatomatic.com/spc/Los-Angeles/Masjid-Omar-Ibn-Al-Khattab/xzyRgn6GN9

Phone for The Halal Businesses Inc., (404) 860-1414 ext. 0

Milton Keynes UK
Ingram Content Group UK Ltd.
UKHW020717090424
440528UK00022B/43

9 798890 317711